W9-AHH-367

HOW
CARBON
FOOTPRINTS
WORK

Nick Hunter

Gareth Stevens
Publishing

Please visit our website, www.garethstevens.com. For a free color catalog of all our high-quality books, call toll free 1-800-542-2595 or fax 1-877-542-2596.

Library of Congress Cataloging-in-Publication Data

Hunter, Nick.
How carbon footprints work / by Nick Hunter.
  p. cm. — (EcoWorks)
Includes index.
ISBN 978-1-4339-9553-8 (pbk.)
ISBN 978-1-4339-9554-5 (6-pack)
ISBN 978-1-4339-9552-1 (library binding)
1. Sustainable living — Juvenile literature. 2. Energy conservation — Juvenile literature. 3. Environmental protection — Juvenile literature. I. Hunter, Nick. II. Title.
G156.5.E26 H86 2014
363.7—dc23

First Edition

Published in 2014 by
Gareth Stevens Publishing
111 East 14th Street, Suite 349
New York, NY 10003

© 2014 Gareth Stevens Publishing

Produced by Calcium, www.calciumcreative.co.uk
Designed by Simon Borrough and Paul Myerscough
Edited by Sarah Eason and Ruth Bennett

Photo credits: Cover: Shutterstock: Fotofactory tr, Risteski Goce b. Inside: Dreamstime: Devy 2, 10, Djembe 11, Flyingdolphin 18, Gbh007 12, Irochka 8, Jlvdream 7, Komelau 9, Maximus117 15, Sabphoto 6, Wimstime 4, Xneo 14; Shutterstock: Abutyrin 22, Dmitry Berkut 25, Lucian Coman 20, Sam Cornwel 16, Dalish 23, Dzinnik Darius 5, Marcio Eugenio 17, Daria Filimonova 27, Innershadows Photography 24, Ixpert 26, Kurhan 13, Bartlomiej Magierowski 21, Mona Makela 1, 29, Fedor Selivanov 19, Ssuaphotos 28.

Printed in the United States of America

CPSIA compliance information: Batch #CS13GS: For further information contact Gareth Stevens, New York, New York at 1-800-542-2595.

Contents

Your Carbon Footprint

If you walk along a beach or a muddy path, you leave a footprint. Footprints in the sand are not the only way in which people leave a mark on their surroundings. We also leave behind an invisible footprint with almost everything that we do. This is our carbon footprint.

What Is a Carbon Footprint?

A carbon footprint is the measurement of how much carbon dioxide and other greenhouse gases are released into the air as a result of your actions. For example, carbon dioxide is released by power plants burning coal and gas to generate electricity, so every time we turn on a light, we cause more carbon to be released.

We cannot see our carbon footprints, but we can measure their effects over long periods of time.

Greenhouse Gases Up Close

Your carbon footprint is not just about carbon dioxide. Other greenhouse gases also cause climate change and these are included in your carbon footprint. Another term for carbon footprint is "carbon dioxide equivalent." Other greenhouse gases include:

- Methane (from farming and landfill): 25 times more harmful than carbon dioxide.
- Nitrous oxide (from industry): 1,000 times more harmful than carbon dioxide.
- Gases, such as sulfur dioxide and propane, (in refrigeration): 1,000 times more harmful than carbon dioxide.

Why Does It Matter?

The size of your carbon footprint matters because the combined footprint of all the people and animals on Earth changes the mixture of gases in the atmosphere. We rely on this mix of gases for the air we breathe, to protect us from the rays of the sun, and to provide the weather conditions that make life possible. There is clear evidence that the carbon footprint of 7 billion human beings on Earth is changing this delicate mix of gases. These gases are called greenhouse gases because they trap heat from the sun and are causing Earth's climate to get warmer.

The food we eat depends on Earth's climate. If it is too hot or too cold, nothing grows.

Carbon Everywhere

Carbon is one of the most important substances on Earth. It makes up less than 0.1 percent of Earth's crust, but it is an essential part of all plants and animals. Carbon is found in the food we grow and eat, as well as in the fuels, such as coal and oil, we burn to give us warmth and to power our industries.

Oxygen from the air reacts with our food to release energy. We breathe out carbon dioxide that is produced in this chemical reaction.

Releasing Carbon

Animals, including humans, release carbon into the atmosphere in the form of carbon dioxide every time they breathe. Carbon dioxide is also released when materials such as wood, oil, and coal are burned. Oil and coal are called fossil fuels because they formed from the remains of prehistoric plants and animals over millions of years. During this time, the carbon inside them was trapped. Burning these fossil fuels releases this carbon into the atmosphere.

Absorbing Carbon

With all these ways of releasing carbon dioxide, why doesn't the atmosphere fill up with carbon? The answer lies in the world's forests and other plants. Plants absorb carbon dioxide through a process called photosynthesis. Huge areas of forest, such as the vast Amazon rain forest in South America, act as the "lungs of Earth."

The Amazon basin of South America is the largest area of tropical rain forest in the world.

Carbon Emissions Up Close

There are two main parts to your carbon footprint:

- Direct carbon emissions: If you use a plastic cup, carbon was directly released in making the cup and shipping it to you, possibly from the other side of the world.
- Indirect carbon emissions: These are caused by all the other people and processes that helped bring the cup to you. They could include mining for the oil that was used to make the plastic in the cup, or the emissions from the luxury car of the person who owns the factory where the cup was made.

The Trouble with Carbon

If carbon is part of all living things, and plants and trees remove it from the atmosphere, why should we worry about our carbon footprint? To answer this question we need to understand the effects of carbon dioxide and other greenhouse gases in the atmosphere.

Coral reefs are home to a huge variety of living things. They are under threat from warming seas and also because absorbed carbon dioxide is changing the oceans.

The Growth of Industry

For most of human history, there was no problem with carbon. The trouble started in the 1700s when factories began to burn coal. At the same time, forests were being cut down to make way for farmland and cities. The levels of carbon dioxide in the atmosphere began to increase.

A Growing Problem

Things got worse in the 1900s, as electricity became the main source of power for homes and factories. Cars, aircraft, and other forms of transportation also developed, and these all used oil-based fuels. Carbon emissions around the world skyrocketed.

More Greenhouse Gases

The increase in carbon emissions has led to a sharp increase in the quantity of greenhouse gases in the atmosphere. These gases trap heat that radiates from Earth's surface, stopping it from being lost in space. As more heat is trapped, the atmosphere gets warmer.

Even small changes in temperature can make a big difference. It can cause large areas of ice in the Arctic and Antarctic to melt. In hotter parts of the world, droughts could be more severe. This would prevent millions of people from growing the food that they need.

If harvests fail because of drought, millions of people will go hungry.

ECO FACT

Temperatures Rising

In 1957, there were 320 parts of carbon dioxide per million in the atmosphere. In just over 50 years, the level of carbon dioxide has risen to almost 400 parts per million. Over the last century, the average surface temperature on Earth has risen by more than 1.3°F (0.7°C).

The World's Carbon Footprint

Scientists say swift action is needed to reduce the carbon footprint of Earth's population and slow the progress of global climate change. But how big a problem is it, and is everyone equally to blame for the rising carbon emissions?

How Much Carbon?

Human activities produce an astonishing 32 billion tons (29 billion mt) of carbon dioxide every year. That's 4 tons (3.6 mt) of carbon dioxide for each man, woman, and child on the planet. Although we know all about the risks of climate change, carbon emissions are still increasing.

Carbon emissions have grown by almost half since 1992. Of course, we don't all have the same-sized carbon footprint. If you're reading this book in the United States, you probably account for more than 4 tons (3.6 mt) of carbon dioxide per year. If you live in Sub-Saharan Africa, however, you probably have a much smaller carbon footprint.

Aircraft are one of the fastest-growing causes of carbon emissions, with air travel expected to grow by 70 percent between 2005 and 2020.

Many people in Africa's poorest countries have almost no carbon emissions as they do not use motorized transportation, electricity, or other sources of carbon.

ECO FACT

Invisible Emissions

The world's carbon emissions are measured in billions of tons. The best way to understand it is with specific examples, especially as we can't see greenhouse gases. For example, a powerful car driven for 1,000 miles (1,600 km) would release around 1 ton (0.9 mt) of carbon dioxide.

The Biggest Footprints

China produces more carbon dioxide than any other country, and was responsible for 8.3 billion tons (7.5 billion mt) in 2010. However, China is also home to more people than any other country. China produces 6 tons (5.4 mt) of carbon dioxide per person, which is well behind the 18 tons (16.3 mt) per person in the United States and Australia. In contrast, many of the world's poorest countries produce fewer than 1 ton (0.9 mt) of carbon dioxide per person. These figures include only direct carbon emissions, and some estimates are much higher.

Calculating Your Carbon

Your own carbon footprint depends on where you live, the transportation you use, how careful you are to limit your electricity use, and even the type of food you eat. One way to calculate your carbon footprint is to keep a diary of everything you do that produces carbon.

The Carbon Culprits

Online carbon calculators help you to get an idea of your carbon footprint. However, they often only consider actions such as direct energy use and transportation, without noting the other ways you produce carbon.

If you can travel to school by bicycle rather than in a car, that will help to reduce your carbon footprint.

How to Reduce Your Carbon Footprint

These are the main areas to think about when trying to reduce your carbon footprint:

- Manufacturing and construction: 38 percent of the average American's carbon footprint is from construction of highways and buildings, which we can't control, and manufacture of the things we buy. The more things you throw away after one use, such as plastic water bottles, the bigger your carbon footprint.
- Personal travel is the next biggest area, with every car or aircraft journey pumping more carbon dioxide into the atmosphere.
- Energy we use at home is another big part of our carbon footprint, particularly heating and air conditioning.
- Farming and food transportation: Has your food been transported from across the world or is it grown near your home, which produces less carbon emissions?

It's hard to think of anything you do that doesn't cause carbon emissions. However, that means there are lots of ways you can reduce your carbon footprint.

Americans buy more than 30 billion bottles of water every year. Producing them uses 17 million barrels of oil and releases 2.5 million tons (2.2 mt) of carbon dioxide.

Farms Up Close

Some foods produce more greenhouse gases than others. Meat produces more carbon than vegetables and grains because animals need energy to live and move around on a farm. If you ate a burger every day, that would produce almost 1 ton (0.9 mt) of carbon dioxide in a year. It wouldn't be very good for your body either!

13

Countering Carbon

Our biggest allies in the fight to reduce our carbon footprint are the trees and plants that absorb carbon. Preserving Earth's precious forests, particularly in tropical regions, is just as important as reducing our own carbon footprints.

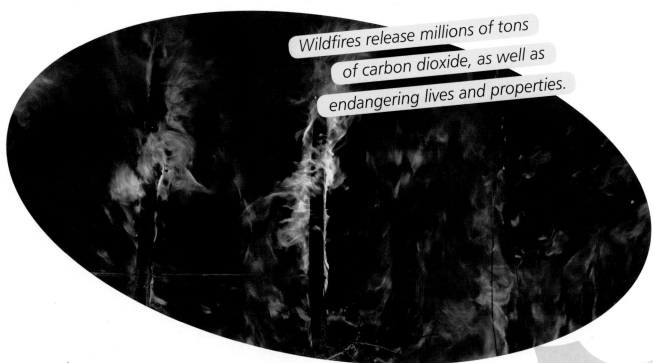

Wildfires release millions of tons of carbon dioxide, as well as endangering lives and properties.

Rain Forests

Tropical rain forests are found in areas close to the equator. They include the Amazon rain forest in South America and other rain forests in Central America, Africa, and Southeast Asia. Tropical rain forests cover about 7 percent of Earth's land area today, but in 1800 they covered twice as much land. Tropical rain forests contain almost half of all the carbon in plants around the world. However, much of these precious forests have been lost to make way for farmland and other human uses.

Burning Rain Forests

When forests are burned, the carbon they contain is released in the form of carbon dioxide, and the area of forest that can absorb carbon is reduced. Preserving this forest is essential to minimize the impact of the human carbon footprint. We can help to preserve rain forests by not buying products made from rain forest trees, such as furniture that is made from mahogany and teak.

Fuels from Crops

Biofuels are crops that can be used as vehicle fuels. Because the plants that make biofuels absorb carbon dioxide while they are growing, they have a lower carbon footprint than fossil fuels. However, to help biocrops grow, fertilizers are used. This releases greenhouse gases into the atmosphere.

More and more land is being used to grow biofuels, but this means there is less space to grow essential food crops.

ECO FACT

Tree Trouble

Trees may not always be the best solution to climate change. In snowy regions, heat from the sun is reflected back into space by the white snow. Planting more trees in these areas could actually increase the pace of climate change, even though the trees absorb carbon from the atmosphere.

Carbon Footprint at Home

Take a look around your home and see if you can find areas where energy is wasted, such as lights or appliances left on in empty rooms. If you can find ways to reduce your family's carbon footprint, you'll probably save some money, too.

Heating and Cooling

Most carbon emissions at home are produced by heating the home and heating water for washing. Heat often escapes through roofs, walls, and drafty windows and doors.

Energy-efficient lightbulbs can reduce our carbon footprint, but not if we leave them on when we don't need them.

Insulation is made from materials that don't allow heat to pass through them easily. Double-glazed windows are also important in preventing heat loss. Air conditioning uses just as much energy as heating but there are other ways to keep your house cool. Tinted or reflective double glazing prevents heat from getting in. Reflective drapes and shades on your windows will also help to keep out the hot sun.

Computers and other electrical appliances have small carbon footprints when compared to heating and air-conditioning systems.

Electrical Appliances

Watching TV for one hour a day produces the same amount of carbon dioxide in a year as a 45-minute journey by car. If you leave the TV on standby the rest of the time, it will actually produce almost as much carbon in a year with no one watching it. If there's a light glowing on the front of a device, then your TV, computer, or any other device is adding to your footprint.

ECO FACT

Brilliant Bulbs

Almost 95 percent of the energy used by an old-fashioned lightbulb is wasted as heat energy. Fluorescent bulbs release less heat so they use less energy and have a smaller carbon footprint.

On the Move

Transportation is one of the main areas where individual choices can make a big difference. Transportation is now the fastest-growing source of greenhouse gas emissions, and about one-third of each American's carbon footprint comes from travel alone.

Car Footprint

Almost all of the 1 billion cars on the roads around the world burn gasoline to provide them with energy. The carbon footprint of your car depends on the size of its engine and the types of trips you take. You could reduce its carbon footprint by making fewer journeys. Could you walk or bike to school?

By reducing your carbon footprint, you will help to protect rain forests and the animals that live in them.

Technology for plug-in hybrid cars is improving all the time. These cars only use a gasoline engine when the charge on their battery runs low.

New Cars Needed

If the world's carbon footprint is to reach manageable levels, new cars are needed. Hybrid cars use an electric motor and a conventional engine to reduce carbon emissions. In the future, most cars could be powered by electricity or clean fuels, such as hydrogen, that produce no carbon dioxide.

Air Travel

If you travel by air, even if it's just once a year, this will make up a big part of your carbon footprint. Aircraft use much more fuel per mile than cars, and people travel farther by plane than they would in a car. A round-trip flight between North America and Europe produces 4 tons (3.6 mt) of carbon for each passenger, which is roughly the same as the average car produces in a year.

Cars Up Close

Here are some tips to reduce the carbon footprint of your car:

- Take as many passengers as possible. The more people there are in the car, the smaller each person's footprint will be.
- Use a smaller car, a hybrid car, or public transportation if you can.
- Try not to travel at busy times. Starting and stopping in busy city traffic can use three times as much energy as driving smoothly.

19

Low-Carbon Shopping

It's easy to see how burning fuel in cars or heating our homes produces carbon dioxide, but what's wrong with shopping? To understand how it affects our carbon footprint, we need to look far beyond the mall.

From Factory to Mall

The biggest contribution to the world's carbon footprint is industry. China, which produces more greenhouse gases than any other country, is also home to the factories that make so many of the consumer goods and clothes you see in your local mall. Metals and other materials need lots of energy to take them out of the ground and refine them for use. Plastics are all made from oil. Manufactured goods also have to be transported across the world for us to buy them.

If more people buy local goods or products with less packaging, this will persuade supermarkets to stock more of these goods.

The 3Rs

There are three main ways to reduce your carbon footprint from shopping:

- Reduce: think about what you need and what you don't need before buying things. Look for goods that have less packaging, as this can use as much energy as the goods themselves.
- Reuse: never buy anything that you use only once. For example, a water bottle can be refilled and used many times.
- Recycle: recycling generally uses less energy than creating entirely new goods. It also cuts down on waste.

Producing goods in China and other countries helps to reduce prices, but there is a price to pay in the carbon footprint of transporting those goods.

ECO FACT

Food Miles

Transporting food produces carbon emissions—particularly perishable food, such as fruit and vegetables. These have to be transported by air to keep them fresh. Strawberries that are flown in from overseas will have 10 times the carbon emissions of any strawberries grown locally and in season.

Carbon Killers

There are many ways that we can each reduce our carbon footprint, but some of the biggest sources of greenhouse gases are beyond the control of individuals. Some of them we can do absolutely nothing about.

Natural Causes

Greenhouse gases are released when anything burns, and some of the biggest explosions on Earth are beyond our control. An erupting volcano produces many millions of tons of carbon emissions. However, it would be misleading to think of volcanoes as contributing to climate change. Big eruptions can change weather over short periods but the carbon produced by volcanoes is fewer than 1 percent of the carbon produced by human activities.

Coal has a bigger carbon footprint than other fuel. Coal use has declined in North America and Europe but is still rising in countries such as China and India.

This geothermal power plant in Iceland heats homes, offices, and even this swimming pool.

ECO FACT

High-Altitude Emissions

We have already seen that air travel is a big contributor to the world's carbon footprint. The full story is even more alarming. Fumes from aircraft produced high in the atmosphere actually have a greater effect on climate than the fumes released at ground level.

Power Problem

The world's carbon footprint could be cut dramatically if countries and power companies changed the fuels that they use to generate electricity. Around two-thirds of electricity in the United States is generated by burning fossil fuels, and in other countries this figure is even higher. Coal is still the number one fuel used by power plants around the world.

Cleaner Energy

Carbon emissions could be reduced by using more natural gas, or, better still, renewable energy, such as solar and wind power. Iceland has abundant supplies of power from hydroelectric dams and geothermal energy from underground, meaning that people can use as much power as they want, whenever they need it, without causing additional and harmful carbon emissions.

Making a Difference?

The world's carbon footprint is so vast that our own part in it can seem insignificant. After all, what's the point of reducing your carbon footprint if more than 1 billion people in China are increasing their carbon dioxide emissions?

If you have space to grow food, this can be rewarding and healthy, as well as reducing the cost and carbon emissions of your food.

Influencing Others

If you decide to reduce your own carbon footprint, you can also convince your friends and other people to do the same. You can find ways to tell people in your school and community about their carbon footprints and suggest steps they can take to cut their impact. You could even suggest ways to reduce your school's carbon footprint.

Changing Others

Just as importantly, your actions can change the way that corporations and governments behave. If corporations see people choosing to buy low-carbon products or driving hybrid cars, they will put more time and money into these products.

Politicians and Pressure Groups

Changes to reduce the carbon footprint of cars and power plants often happen because of government laws. You can write to local or national representatives about taking steps to reduce carbon emissions. There are also many nongovernmental organizations and pressure groups that work to tackle carbon emissions and inform people about the issue.

ECO FACT

Some people feel so strongly about climate change and pollution that they join pressure groups to make their views heard.

Predicting the Future

Scientists have no doubts that climate change is happening, but predicting how much carbon we will produce in the future and what effect it will have is much more difficult. The Intergovernmental Panel on Climate Change has predicted that global temperatures could rise by anywhere between 2°F and 11°F (1.1°C and 6.4°C) by 2099.

Carbon Trading and Offsetting

Carbon trading is one way that the world's governments have tried to reduce carbon emissions. It means that businesses now have to pay for the greenhouse gases they produce. Businesses and individuals can also offset, or make up for, their own greenhouse gas emissions.

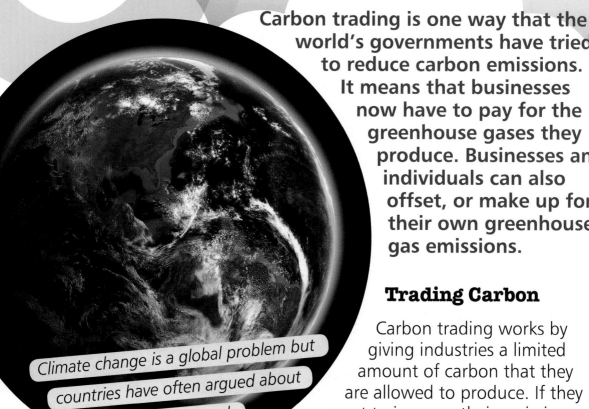

Climate change is a global problem but countries have often argued about how they should work together to solve it.

Trading Carbon

Carbon trading works by giving industries a limited amount of carbon that they are allowed to produce. If they want to increase their emissions, they have to buy credits from another business that has not used all its credits. This rewards industries and countries that take steps to try to reduce their carbon emissions.

Offsetting

Many businesses try to reduce their carbon footprints by offsetting the carbon they produce. Ways to do this include paying for trees to be planted, which will help to absorb the carbon dioxide. It can also mean putting money into renewable energy—such as by distributing energy-saving lightbulbs in developing countries.

Tree Planting

Some businesses, such as airlines, will give customers the option to pay toward tree planting to offset the extra carbon emissions of their flight. While carbon offsetting may well be better than no action at all, critics say that it doesn't really tackle the main issue of developing lifestyles and technology less dependent on carbon.

Planting a tree makes your local environment nicer and may help to offset your carbon footprint.

Carbon Offsetting Up Close

Carbon offsetting may make people feel better about choosing to take a long-haul flight, but does it really make any difference? Problems with offsetting include:

- It may take a very long time for trees that are planted to absorb the carbon dioxide that is being produced.
- If we are to reduce our carbon footprint, offsetting should happen in addition to reducing carbon emissions, not instead of it.

Footprints in the Future

We now understand more than ever before about the invisible footprint that we leave on the planet. However, we are still a long way from slowing the pace of climate change. The race is now on to find new ways of reducing the world's carbon footprint before it's too late.

Future Power

Power plants are still heavily reliant on fossil fuels. Wind, wave, and solar energy are all ways of generating electricity with almost no carbon footprint, but these sources currently provide only a very small amount of our energy. One solution to this problem is to build giant solar power plants to be powered by the constant sunshine in desert regions, or make solar panels part of every new building.

Huge areas covered with wind turbines would be needed if wind energy were to provide more than a small part of our energy needs.

New Technology

Scientists are also working on technology to capture the carbon produced by our fossil-fuel power plants and store it underground so it does not reach the atmosphere.

Carbon-Free Cars

New materials will also help to reduce the carbon footprint of the average car. Much of the energy a car uses is to push the vehicle itself, rather than the people or luggage it carries. Scientists are working at a microscopic level to create ultra-light but strong materials for the next generation of cars. These cars will be powered by plug-in electric motors or even by hydrogen fuel cells, producing no carbon emissions.

New buildings can use high-tech or natural materials to provide insulation and reduce their carbon emissions.

ECO FACT

Future Challenges

Earth's population is expected to rise from the 7 billion people on the planet in 2012 to 9 billion people by 2050. The challenge is to keep our carbon footprint at the same level as today, or even to lower it, with 2 billion more people on the planet.

Glossary

atmosphere a layer of gases surrounding Earth and containing the oxygen that humans and other animals breathe

carbon dioxide (CO$_2$) a greenhouse gas that is released when fossil fuels and organic matter are burned

carbon footprint the amount of greenhouse gas emissions caused by a single person or organization

carbon trading a system by which businesses have a fixed allowance of carbon emissions that they can trade with others

conventional normal or usual, such as conventional cars powered by an internal combustion engine

developing countries countries where most people have a low standard of living, and modern industry and their economies are still developing

fossil fuels energy sources formed from the decayed remains of living things, including coal, oil, and natural gas

gasoline a flammable product made from crude oil that is used to power engines

generate to create or produce

geothermal having to do with heat and energy from beneath Earth's crust

greenhouse gases gases that absorb heat in the atmosphere

hybrid car a car that has two sources of power, such as an electric motor and a conventional gasoline engine

hydrogen a flammable gas that combines with oxygen to make water

insulation material that does not conduct heat and can prevent heat energy from escaping, such as from a building

refrigeration the process of keeping things cool, such as food

renewable able to be replaced by natural processes. Solar energy, for example, is renewable.

solar from the sun

For More Information

Books

Doeden, Matt. *Green Energy: Crucial Gains or Economic Strains*. Breckenridge, CO: Twenty-First Century Books, 2010.

Nagle, Jeanne. *Smart Shopping: Shopping Green*. New York, NY: Rosen Central, 2008.

Rooney, Anne. *Reducing the Carbon Footprint*. London, UK: Franklin Watts, 2009.

Townsend, John. *Predicting the Effects of Climate Change*. Mankato, MN: Heinemann-Raintree, 2008.

Websites

Find out more about carbon at:
www.sciencekids.co.nz/sciencefacts/ chemistry/carbon.html

This carbon footprint calculator works out your carbon footprint based on some of the most common ways we use energy:
www.cooltheworld.com/kidscarboncalculator.php

Check out the Environmental Protection Agency's climate change site at:
www.epa.gov/climatestudents/index.html

Publisher's note to educators and parents: Our editors have carefully reviewed these websites to ensure that they are suitable for students. Many websites change frequently, however, and we cannot guarantee that a site's future contents will continue to meet our high standards of quality and educational value. Be advised that students should be closely supervised whenever they access the Internet.

Index